Linda A. Brown

MONSTERS OF THE MIDDLE AGES

About the Book

Did you know that the horn of a Unicorn has magic in it? That mermaids have been seen combing their hair as they ride between the waves? Or that dragons love gold and try to hide great piles of it? People long ago believed all these things! William Wise tells us the fantastic tales that people in the Middle Ages made up to explain the things that frightened them. And Tomie de Paola has brought these colorful medieval monsters humorously to life.

MONSTERS
of the Middle Ages

by William Wise

Illustrated by Tomie de Paola

G. P. Putnam's Sons
·
New York

Library of Congress Catalog Card Number: 72-145455

PRINTED IN THE UNITED STATES OF AMERICA
06208

Second Impression

SBN: GB 399-60472-3

Long before our own day, there was a time called the Middle Ages. Much of the world had not yet been discovered by the explorers. People in Europe did not even know there *was* a land that would later be called America.

Life during the Middle Ages was very
different from what it is today. It was a time
when kings and queens lived in stone castles. It
was a time when knights went into battle
wearing suits of armor. If they went into battle
on horseback, their horses wore armor, too.

Most men, though, were not kings or knights.
Some were peasants, who lived in small villages.
Some were craftsmen or merchants, who lived
in small towns.

During the Middle Ages most people never went far from their homes. The roads were bad, so it was not easy to travel. There were no cars or airplanes to take people quickly from one place to another.

If a man had to travel, he usually rode a horse. Or he rode a donkey. If he was too poor to own a horse or a donkey, he went on foot.

Because most people stayed near home, they knew very little about the rest of the world. This was one reason why they believed in many stories that today we know are not true.

THE WORLD

People in the Middle Ages believed that the world was filled with monsters. They liked to hear stories about strange men and animals that were said to live in far-off lands. These stories sound foolish now. But they did not sound foolish to people in the Middle Ages.

One story told of a country called Abarimon.
The people of Abarimon were said to have
their feet turned backward.

You might think they could not get around
very well, with their feet turned backward. But
the story said they were such fast runners that
no one else could keep up with them!

Other strange men were called the Monocoli. They each had only one leg, but they got around very well, too — by jumping!

They jumped so fast and so far that even a man with two legs could not hope to catch them.

Then there were the Astomi, who were said to live in faraway India. They did not eat or drink, like other people. Instead, they fed themselves by smelling flowers!

Sometimes, when a traveler came home, he liked to tell tales about his adventures. Sir John Mandeville was a great teller of tales.

On one faraway island, Sir John said he had
found some Giants. He said they were twenty
feet tall. They wore clothing made of animal
skins and ate meat without cooking it.

Sir John had heard about other Giants, who lived on a different island. He had not seen them. But he had been told they were seventy-five feet tall! They kept very big sheep, too. Such giant sheep must have given a great deal of wool. Sir John had wanted to catch a few to bring back home. Unluckily, though, he hadn't been able to find even one!

Many monsters of the Middle Ages were said to be part man and part animal. One of them was the Manticore. He was supposed to live far away in the East. He had the head of a man and the body of a lion. Some people said he also had the tail of a scorpion.

The Manticore must have been an ugly monster. He had three rows of teeth and ate any animal he could catch. If he caught a man, the Manticore ate him, too.

The only pleasant thing about the Manticore was his voice. It was beautiful. It sounded like a flute.

The Lamia was a monster that lived in Africa. People believed she was part woman and part snake. Her voice was *not* beautiful. It sounded like the hiss of a snake.

The Lamia could run very quickly. It was said that she was always hungry and would eat any animal or man that crossed her path.

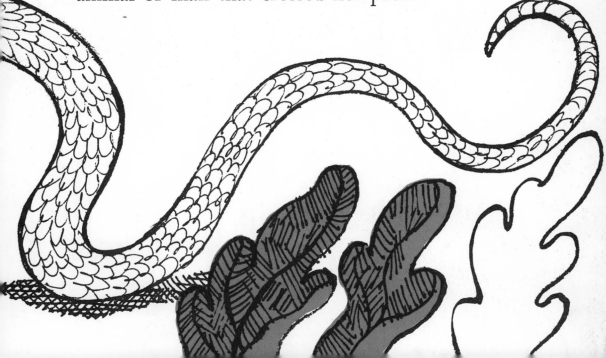

The Centaur was a strange monster, with the head of a man and the body of a horse. His voice sounded like the whinny of a horse. And he could run as fast as a horse.

In some ways, though, the Centaur acted like a man. He hunted with a bow and arrows. And when he felt sad, the Centaur cried.

Still, he was not a friendly monster. Whenever people wandered into the deep woods where he lived, he tried to shoot them with his arrows.

During the Middle Ages, people did not know much about the way wild animals lived. They were afraid of many creatures, especially snakes. So they made up fantastic stories about them.

The Amphisbaena was one of the made-up snakes. He was said to have a head at each end of his body. People believed that you never could catch the Amphisbaena off guard. For when one of his heads was sleeping, the other head was always awake.

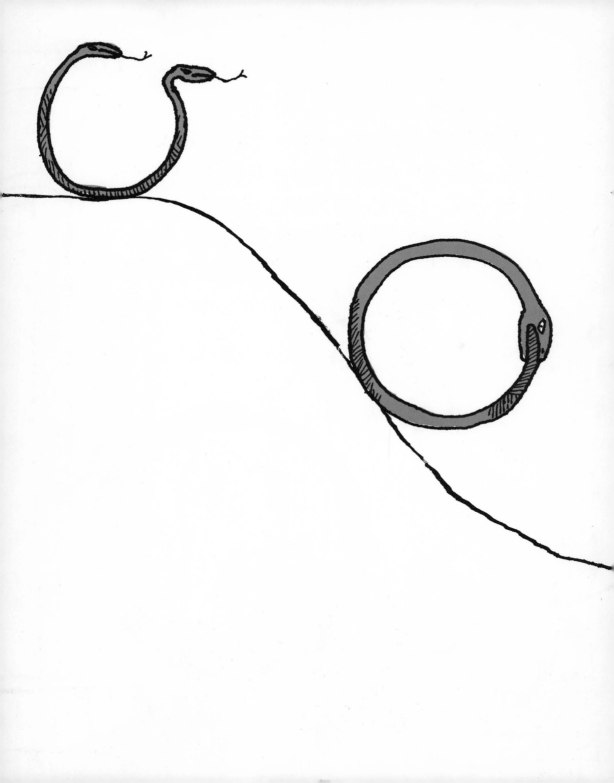

People also believed that the Amphisbaena could crawl just as fast, backward or forward. When he came to the top of a hill, he did a strange thing. He put one head inside the other. Then he rolled down the hill, just like a hoop!

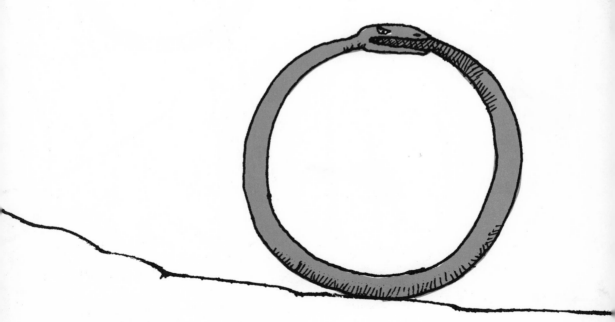

The Basilisk was a snake that lived where it was very hot. To people in the Middle Ages, he was the king of all monster snakes.

There were many ways a Basilisk could kill his enemies. His terrible smell was enough to do it. And the hissing sound he made was so frightening that many animals died of terror when they heard it.

Of course, the bite of the Basilisk would kill an animal at once. But so much heat came out of his mouth that most animals were killed even *before* he could bite them.

And that wasn't all. The eye of the Basilisk was truly horrible. If a man looked into it for just a second or two, he fell over dead.

After hearing stories like that, it was no wonder people kept away from any real snakes they might see in the fields or along the road.

Almost everyone believed in Dragons during
the Middle Ages. Some Dragons had wings and
could fly through the air. Others had no wings
and stayed on the ground.

Some Dragons had feet, but many did not.
The ones without feet looked very much like
snakes.

A few Dragons were said to be friendly. But most were not. They breathed flames and fire and were thought to eat large numbers of people whenever they got the chance.

Often a dangerous Dragon lived in a cave.
He might hide his gold there, for Dragons
were supposed to love gold.

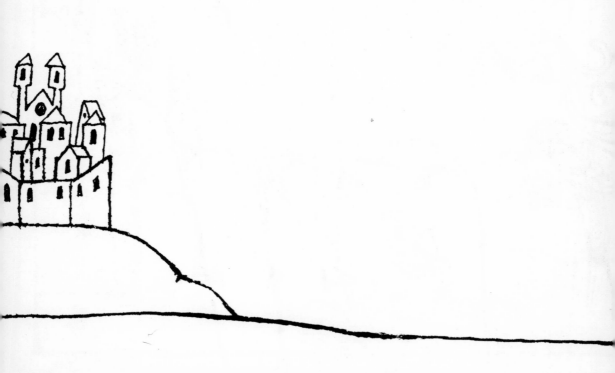

Or the Dragon might kidnap a princess and keep her inside his cave until her father, the king, paid a ransom of gold to get her back. In many stories, a young knight would put on his suit of armor. Then he would ride off to the cave, to fight the Dragon.

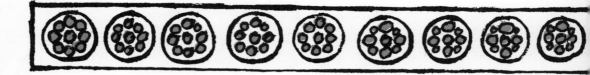

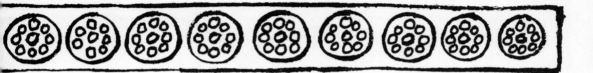

The young knight usually won the battle. Then he would find the gold and the princess. Having rescued the princess, he would take her home to her father, the king. Before long the knight and the princess would get married. At the end of the story they would become king and queen.

All during the Middle Ages, sailors liked to talk about their adventures. Sometimes they really did see strange-looking animals, whose names we know today. But when the sailors got back home and told their stories, these odd-looking animals often sounded like dangerous monsters.

Many sailors claimed they had seen a Mermaid while at sea. The Mermaid was supposed to be half woman and half fish. She had long hair, which she liked to comb as she rode between the waves. Sailors believed their ship would sink, if it got too close to a Mermaid.

Probably the Mermaid was just a large animal we called the sea cow. You can still find sea cows today. They are big, gentle creatures that do not harm anyone.

The Su was a monster that lived near the southern seas. Sailors said that she had an amazing tail. It was almost as long as her body. When she saw a ship, she put her children on her back and covered them with her tail.

The Su probably was a real animal. But from the tales the sailors told about her, it is hard to guess which wild animal she really was.

The Kraken was a sea monster of the north. In some stories, he pulled a man over the ship's side and carried him under the waves. In other stories, the Kraken attacked a ship and sank it, drowning all but one of the crew.

Few of these stories could have been true. But the Kraken *was* a real animal — a giant squid. He still can be found in the sea. He is one of the largest creatures in the world.

One of the most famous stories told in the
Middle Ages was about the Unicorn. He was a
white animal with a long horn. No man could
catch the Unicorn by chasing him. But if a
beautiful young woman were left alone in the
woods, the Unicorn would come and put his
head in her lap. Then he would fall asleep, and
men could come and capture him.

People believed that the horn of the Unicorn had magic in it. They thought that if they ground up some of the horn and ate it, they would be safe from snakebite. They thought they even would be safe from the bite of a Basilisk!

The horn of the Unicorn looked a little bit like the horn of two real animals — the rhinoceros, which still lives in Africa, and the narwhal, which still lives in the northern seas.

But the Unicorn did not look like them in other respects. When he was shown in pictures, he looked like a white horse, with a horn, a goat's beard, and the tail of a lion.

Today no one believes that there are any Unicorns hiding in the woods. No one believes that there are any Mermaids swimming in the sea or Dragons flying through the air.

Today we know there really are no such creatures. But for many, many years, people did believe in them — and in all the other amazing monsters of the Middle Ages.

KEY WORDS

adventure(s)

armor

castle(s)

craftsmen

dangerous

explorer(s)

fantastic

flute

hiss

kidnap

knights

merchant(s)

Middle Ages

monster(s)

narwhal

peasant(s)

ransom

rhinoceros

scorpion

sea cow

squid

whinny

The Monsters:

Abarimon (men of)

Amphisbaena

Astomi

Basilisk

Centaur

Dragon

Giant

Kraken

Lamia

Manticore

Mermaid

Monocoli

Su

Unicorn

The Author

WILLIAM WISE is the prizewinning author of more than a dozen books for young readers. His books on exciting creatures of fact and fiction include *In the Time of the Dinosaurs, The World of Giant Mammals, Monsters of the Ancient Seas, Monsters of Today and Yesterday, The Amazing Animals of Latin America, The Amazing Animals of Australia,* and, most recently, *The Amazing Animals of North America.* Among his many books for older children are *The Two Reigns of Tutankhamen,* which received a Boys' Clubs of America Junior Book Award Medal, and *Alexander Hamilton,* a Junior Literary Guild Selection.

The Artist

TOMIE DE PAOLA was born in Connecticut and has degrees in fine arts from Pratt Institute and the California College of Arts and Crafts. His artistic talents have displayed themselves in many areas: book illustration, greeting card and stationery design, theater design, and church crucifixes, murals, and vestments. To date, he has some twenty children's books to his credit, several of which he both wrote and illustrated. His most recently illustrated book for Putnam's is the picture book *Rutherford T. Finds 21 B.*

Some selected See and Read books:

In the Time of the Dinosaurs
by William Wise • Illustrated by Lewis Zacks

The World of Giant Mammals
by William Wise • Illustrated by Lewis Zacks

Monsters of Today and Yesterday
by William Wise • Illustrated by Lee Smith

Monsters of the Ancient Seas
by William Wise • Illustrated by Joseph Sibal

Giant Birds and Monsters of the Air
by William Wise • Illustrated by Joseph Sibal

The Amazing Animals of Latin America
by William Wise • Illustrated by Joseph Sibal

The Amazing Animals of Australia
by William Wise • Illustrated by Joseph Sibal

Giant Snakes and Other Amazing Reptiles
by William Wise • Illustrated by Joseph Sibal

The Amazing Animals of North America
by William Wise • Illustrated by Joseph Sibal